Assertiveness at Work

How to Become More Assertive At Work and Take Control

(Volume 2)

Lauren Bates

CONTENTS

PUBLISHERS NOTES

ISBN: 978-1-939643-19-3

First Published In United States 2010 And Licensed For Republication By Speedy Publishing LLC on March 2013.

Speedy Publishing LLC

40 East Main Street, No. 725,

Newark, DE 19711-4639

Paperback Edition 2013

For information about special discounts for bulk purchases, please contact Speedy Publishing Sales Department at 646-312-7900 or publishing@speedypublishing.com

Manufactured in the United States of America

Disclaimer

Lauren Bates

This publication is intended to provide helpful and informative material. It is not intended to diagnose, treat, cure, or prevent any health problem or condition, nor is intended to replace the advice of a physician. No action should be taken solely on the contents of this book. Always consult your physician or qualified health-care professional on any matters regarding your health and before adopting any suggestions in this book or drawing inferences from it.

The author and publisher specifically disclaim all responsibility for any liability, loss or risk, personal or otherwise, which is incurred as a consequence, directly or indirectly, from the use or application of any contents of this book.

Any and all product names referenced within this book are the trademarks of their respective owners. None of these owners have sponsored, authorized, endorsed, or approved this book.

Always read all information provided by the manufacturers' product labels before using their products. The author and publisher are not responsible for claims made by manufacturers.

To Ralph and Maria - Be patient; your business will improve if you keep at it. The information here is for you.

CHAPTER 1- HOW TO KEEP YOURSELF INVOLVED IN ASSERTIVENESS TRAINING

When you are looking to find ways to improve your life, you may want to think about how assertive you are. This is a good trait that you may want to have in order to find ways to make your life better. Getting to be assertive is something that many people do not know how to do the right way. You need to have some involvement in assertiveness training to keep motivated.

The training that you will receive for assertiveness is based on a multilevel method. There is a set of verbal skills that you will need to learn as well as your way of thinking. There are different situations that we all have to deal with on a regular basis. Having good assertive training will help us deal with these situations and make the right choices for our own lives.

You have to stay comfortable with your assertiveness training. You need to make sure that you are feeling good about the way that it is taking place. You should like the instructors and the people that are helping you with your assertiveness. When you use the methods that you learn from your training, you will see big changes in the way that you live your life and the way that others treat you too. Gaining respect and being respectful are the two most important reasons to be assertive.

There are different practices for being assertive. You should think about what is going to be more important to you and go from there. If you are having a hard time figuring out what you need to do to be more assertive, ask your trainer. You should feel free to ask as many questions as you need so that you are in complete understanding of how you should act.

Assertiveness At Work

Once you start the assertiveness training, you will see the difference. You will notice that you are more comfortable speaking in front of others and making your own opinions known. You will have the ability to let others see you for who you are and how you think about certain things. There is nothing wrong with having your own feelings about things. You will be able to express these feeling more openly and be more honest with yourself as well.

After you see the improvement that you have been making on your life, you will want to keep continuing with your assertiveness training. You will want to use your skills in this course to keep on getting what you want out of life and being more open with others about anything. You will also see how others are taking notice in you and how they want to hear what you have to say. The assertiveness training is something that you will want to continue to do for as long as you feel the need.

Do not let what you have learned from your assertiveness training courses be forgotten. You want to keep on going with everything that you have learned and use it in your daily life. You do not have to be a push over anymore. You can learn to say no when you want to and feel good about it afterwards. You should use your method of assertiveness to take control over your life. This is going to be a life changing experience for most and it is something that many need to do in order to be happier. Do not forget everything that you have put into being a more assertive person and use it to your advantage any time you feel the need.

CHAPTER 2- ASSERTIVENESS TRAINING AND GETTING YOUR POINT ACROSS

When you want to get your point across, you need to make sure that you are assertive and have the right training to do so. You want others to hear what you have to say and feel as if you are important. This is something that you should think about anytime you are speaking in front of an audience.

Do not be afraid to express your feelings. It makes no difference if you are in a public setting or just in front of some friends. You have to make sure that you are doing what you need to so that you are taken seriously. There are so many people that are not secure in the way that they feel. However feeling confident and secure in your own skin is very crucial to the way that you react to others.

You need to be confident and have great self-esteem. There is nothing wrong with wanting to feel important. You have to make sure that you are using your assertiveness training and doing what you feel in the moment. Getting to be assertive may be something that you already know how to do. If you do not, you should use assertiveness training to get you where you want to be.

You can get assertiveness training online or off. There are plenty of different ways to get the assertiveness training and feel confident in whom you are and what you do in life. You need to make sure that you are doing what you need to so that you have all the confidence in yourself. There is nothing that should stand in your way. When you are assertive and use it to get your point across, you will get others to hear you and notice what you have to say.

Take your time and think about what you want others to know. Make sure that you are being assertive and using your skill to make others want to listen to all the things that you have to say. You need to think about what is most important to you and how you feel. Take your opportunities and use them when you can. There is nothing wrong with wanting to be more confident. This is especially true when you are doing all that you can to get others to stand up and take notice of you.

Working on your assertiveness and doing all that you can to make yourself feel more confident and use all that you have learned from your assertiveness training is important. Do not be afraid to out there and make things happen for yourself. You have to do what you can to make others hear your point and take it seriously. There is nothing wrong with wanting to have the attention of others and feel as if you are getting your point across and others can hear what you want them to know.

Be consistent and know what you are talking about. Get all the facts and incorporate them into what you want others to know. You need to express how you feel so that others can hear what you want them to know. Do not be self-conscious and stand up for yourself. You have to take charge of your life and make sure that other feels the same way. Show them that it is assertiveness that makes you feel better about whom you are. With you being assertive, you can teach others this great quality and help them stand up for themselves and get the self-esteem that they need.

CHAPTER 3- HOW TO BE MORE ASSERTIVE AND INCREASE YOUR SELF ESTEEM

There are so many ways that you can become assertive and increase your self-esteem. There are lots of things that will help you to become assertive, but you have to find something that you love. Once you find something that you love you'll find that the assertiveness and eagerness to go after it will push you. It is the natural way of learning how to be more assertive because you have the feelings that push you to do whatever it takes to get what you want. One you get what you want you'll find that your self-esteem will also increase. This will help you increase your self-esteem because you are seeing the rewards of your hard work.

If you can't find something that motivates you, you may find someone to help motivate you and you'll become more assertive because of it. It's like you care so much about the person that they have a direct effect on how you feel about things. You'll find motivation in your need to make them happy. This may not be the best way to get assertive; however, it will increase your self-esteem when you see the person's face. Some people are lucky to have others that motivate them to find something that they want. They are very lucky people who have someone to give them some direction because otherwise you may get lost.

For those who are lost, you may just need to do a trial and error thing. This is because you may not know what you want so you'll have to play around until you find something that strikes your fancy. You may end up doing tons of crafts, changing jobs, and disrupting your entire life because you are trying to find something that will get you going. There are some people who need the motivation and there are some people who just are assertive.

Assertiveness At Work

For those people who are just assertive they find motivation in a lot of things. They find motivation in money, in love, and even some competition. Competition is a great motivator. You'll find that not only will get you to become more assertive but it will also increase your self-esteem. You will find that when you get your heart into something you'll feel ten times better about yourself. You'll also feel better because there is something that you really desire. You have a goal and when you have goals you will find that your-self-image will look a lot better because your happy, your motivated, and you're on top of the game.

If you really want to become assertive you may want to take some small steps on your own. At work, get your boss a cup of coffee. They will then notice that you took the assertiveness to do something that you weren't told and then they will begin to notice you. Assertive people are the ones that get the promotions. They are the ones that get the big bucks because they know how to work it. You will want to do some so stuff and eventually it will come natural to you. Then you will be the one that everyone is noticing and that will do a lot for your self-esteem.

It's not hard to see a link between your self-esteem and your level of assertiveness. You will find that the results of your assertiveness will make you feel good about yourself. You will want to become assertive so that you too can be recognized as a hard worker. It's hard t get noticed, but if you take the time to show your boss that you are assertive, they will notice and appreciate your work.

CHAPTER 4- HOW TO BE MORE ASSERTIVE AND OUTGOING

It's hard to become more assertive, especially if you are a shy person. For those who don't have the outgoing personality that comes natural to some people, you will find that being more assertive can be a challenge, however, if you take the time you'll be able to find the right times to show your more aggressive side and you'll be able to become more assertive naturally. For those who wish to become more assertive you need to find something that you really like and then reach out for it. You need to become more outgoing when it comes to your relationships, your friendships, and your career.

When it comes to having a serious relationship you may want to talk to your girlfriend or friend about taking the friendship further. You can take some measures that will seem to protect your feelings. If you don't want to talk directly, you will find a lot of pressure gone when you write them a note or an email. You'll feel more confident talking to them about the relationship when the conversation goes one way. You're being outgoing by trying to go for something that you really want, but you are also being assertive because you are stating your feelings without being asked for them. You will find that this will help you to become more assertive when it comes to getting into relationships and you'll be more outgoing when in the relationships.

When it comes to your friendships you may find security in the friendship. When you feel secured you'll become more assertive. For those who feel like they have nothing to lose, they are more likely to go for things, they are more likely to express themselves when they feel secure with the person. There I no reason why you shouldn't be assertive and outgoing if you feel secured in the friendship or relationship to be yourself.

Assertiveness At Work

The career is very different. You may never feel secured in your career. You will have to find a reason for you to become more assertive, like it is part of a plan. This is because for you to be secured in your career you have to become more assertive and outgoing for management and the upper bosses to notice you. If you work at a company that hardly even knows your name then you should try to be more assertive and outgoing just so that you can get recognized as a member of the company. You may even want to talk to your supervisor or department head so that you can find tips on how to work your way up in the company and how you encourage yourself to become assertive and more outgoing.

You really shouldn't be shy when it comes to meeting new people. You will find that when it comes to new people you may end up making a lot of new friendships. The best part of meeting new people is that you can be whoever you want to be, and that includes being yourself. You don't have to worry about meeting new expectations of others. You will make a lot of new friends because you'll be so confident and outgoing since you'll be comfort being yourself.

You also shouldn't be shy when it comes to new experiences. If you allow your mind to be open to new experiences you may be able to make a huge difference to your life. You may be able to find something that will make you happy or have a positive outlook on your life. When you are open to new experiences you will be able to enlighten your life and become assertive and outgoing.

CHAPTER 5- HOW TO BE MORE ASSERTIVE WHILE TRAINING NEW EMPLOYEES

It is hard training new employees; however, it's even harder to be assertive when training new employees. Before you meet the new ones you are going to have to give yourself a pep talk. You were the one that was given the task of training because you highly know what you are doing. Don't worry about your qualifications because your boss already thinks you'll be a good leader to the group. You should also know that it is a great honor for you train your new employees. As for the assertiveness, most people lose assertiveness and control over the group because they lack confidence. Do you think that someone will pay more attention to someone who knows exactly what they are doing or someone who is passive and not sure of themselves? You have to seem like you are in charge. You have to give all the information with authority. That means you have to make sure that everything that you say is said with authority and a tone that is strong and in charge.

If you are trying to be more assertive throughout the orientation with the new employees you will want to start off by leading the group and getting to know each other. Have everyone introduce themselves and then say a little bit of their role with the company. You will also want to start things off with an ice breaker. You will find that if you tell the group a little bit about yourself and how you have become successful within the company, you'll be able to bond with the group and feel more comfortable showing assertiveness with them. Also, get to know them by asking some questions, small talk. This will allow you to feel more comfortable with the new employees and you'll find that your assertiveness will grow as you become comfortable.

You should also come to the group with a certain bit of attitude. Like if you find yourself coming into the situation with confidence you will feel a lot better about the situation and you'll slow the new employees how assertive you truly are. You will want to come into the situation with a lot of confidence because you'll feel better. Even if you fake it for a while, you'll be able to find yourself confident in being the lead role. You should feel honored that you were given the job, and you'll also find that if you feel like you got this down you'll be able to become an even better leader. When it comes to talking to groups of people it's like being around dogs; they can smell your fear. If you come into the group with fear written all over your face, you'll find that none of the people will respect you.

You may even want to ask your boss for a pep talk. The boss will tell you that you are capable of talking in front of the group and they will also tell you why you make such a great role model for the new employees. Use all of that information for your own good. With the pep talk you should be able to walk out and greet them with confidence. Once you have found your confidence you can show others how assertive you can be. Remember, assertive people are not demanding or seem too proud. Assertive people know exactly what needs to said and done so that the company can progress positively.

There are so many ways that you can generate assertiveness within yourself, however, you should allow others to support you so that you feel more confident and qualified to do the job and do the job right.

CHAPTER 6- HOW TO BE MORE ASSERTIVE AND SAY NO

There are lot of kids that have had to grow up doing whatever their friends pressured them to do because they were not assertive enough to say no. They end up getting themselves in a lot of trouble because they are unable to say no. When it comes to teaching your child to become assertive and say no, you have to show that you are not being judgmental, but that you just care about how they are raised. If you talk to your child you will be able to get assertiveness to grow inside them so that they know better than to not say no. They will end up being well-adjusted and mature young adults, but it's not just kids and teens that have issues with saying no. There are a lot more times in life when you are going to need to say no, but you may feel like you can't.

The first type of situation where you may feel like you aren't assertive enough to say no is at work. The problem is that if you say no you may find others to have issues with your unwillingness. Some employees are required to convert to the regular office standards and seem less than willing to negotiate. Honestly, if you can be true to your job you will be able to keep your job, impress the boss, and still be able to feel free to say no. Sometimes you'll feel pressured to take on more work, even if you have plans or cannot take on the extra work, but if you tell your boss the circumstances you'll be more likely to be noticed for your assertiveness, however, you have to set your priorities. You should always put your family first. You will find the assertiveness inside you to say no because you know what needs to be done for the sake of your family, your career, and stability. You will become assertive because you will understand what you need to do to make things work and sometimes it means to say no to the big bosses.

Assertiveness At Work
The second type of situation that you may feel pressured is when you are in a relationship. You may feel that you can't say no to someone, but that is not the type of relationship that you should have. There are always times in life when you feel the need to say no. There are going to be topics in which you'll feel the need to put your foot down and tell them that their wishes are out of control. You may end finding your assertiveness after giving the other partner so much that it is physically exhausting, however, you may also find that you will be able to share the partnership from the start equally. Love means that there is a give and an take. Not just one person is doing all the giving and that is where you will want to find the assertiveness. You will want to become more assertive for the fact that the other will never respect you. You will want to have the mutual respect and if you feel like you honestly cannot say no to them then you will want to have and talk about the relationship. This is the only way that you may be able to gain some respect in the relationship and also become more assertive so that the relationship is equal.

The last type of situation where you may feel pressured is much like when you were a teen. You'll find that others will try to persuade you to do things that you shouldn't do. You, again, can find some real trouble by associating with these people, but fear alone will not give you the nerve to say no. You have to become comfortable with who you are before you can tell others how you feel about things and take a stand against the crowd.

Chapter 7- How To Be More Assertive And Develop A Positive Attitude

Being positive is very hard to do and it sometimes takes more than just assertiveness for you to become positive, but if you are able to find assertive attitudes then you'll be able to have a positive attitude. The key to being assertive is being focused. You will begin to lose your drive when you lose your focus, but if you are able to see your goals in the small picture form and the larger picture form you'll always be assertive or driven to reach such goals.

There are no written rules on how you can become more assertive. In fact, rather you are assertive or not will depend on the type of home you were raised in and what type of personality that you have. Those who are more outgoing and positive are more assertive and those who are assertive are more positive. This is because you don't see the "I-can'ts" but you see "how can". You see things in a more positive light. There are people who are naturally assertive and then there are people who lack the positive attitude to be assertive. For you to really show your assertive side you have to be very comfortable with the situation that you are in. You have to be comfortable with the people who you are communicating with and dealing with. You have to be comfortable with your surroundings. You also have to become comfortable with yourself.

The first step for you to become a better person and more assertive you have to work on yourself. You have to become comfortable with yourself and with who you are. You will have to be able to look at yourself and see something positive. You will have to keep a positive attitude about yourself if you really want to show others how assertive you are. You will never have the nerve to be assertive about anything if you cannot appreciate the world and yourself.

You should also know that you will never be assertive if there is no one to believe in your dreams, your goals, and within you that you can do anything. You need to have someone to believe in you to make things seem so easy to obtain. You need to have someone who can appreciate everything that you do and everything that you wish to do. You should also think about having a support system. There are always people around you to help you gain the assertiveness needed to reach all of your dreams and goals. For you to be assertive you need to be driven, and the people around you are just some of the things that may drive you to become a better person or drive you to reach your goals.

Once you believe in yourself and you have someone to believe in you, you'll find that you'll change. You'll become a totally different person This is because you have a sparkle in your eye. You have a goal that you need to reach and the support from others to reach your goals. Believing in yourself can do a lot for a person's career, personal life, and general good health.

For you to become assertive and positive you have to find confidence from accepting yourself for who you are and accepting others around you for who they are. You will also want to lean on the shoulders of others when you feel like you are getting off track. When you are confident in yourself you will show others your confidence and assertiveness. You will also increase the positive things in your life by becoming more assertive.

CHAPTER 8- ASSERTIVENESS FOR MANAGER'S SUCCESS

It can be very difficult for you to be a manager, but it is even more difficult to show your assertiveness to your follow workers and employees. It is hard because you are being placed in a situation where you are the boss, but you would also like to bond with your employees and be friends. Sometimes the boss is not always your friend, but they can always show respect to all employees.

The first thing that you have to recognize is that you are the manager and you have a role of being a role model to others and you also have to recognize that you have a duty to serve as guidance to others. Once you realize that your employees are not just your friends, but they are your workers, you'll feel better about being more assertive about the orders. You will feel a lot better about your job if you become assertive and firm with the rules. As a manager, your role is to make sure that your workers have everything done on time and correctly. You will want to find the assertiveness to get your workers motivated and even pitch in so everything is done, if you don't, then you have a chance of losing your job. The fear of losing your job will motivate anyone to take the opportunity to help out.

When it comes to being assertive you are going to find that you need to be assertive by caring for your workers and by helping them out when you need to. First, you need to be assertive as a manager to care for your workers. When you see that one of your works is having a bad day, you have to talk to them and communicate the situation with them so that they can work harder. You will also want to care for your employees and show them courtesy so that they will feel comfortable coming to you when there is an issue at work. If you keep the channels of communication open you'll be able to have more productive workers. The second thing is that you have to make sure that the work gets done on time before overtime is given out. You may find yourself in a lot of trouble if you can't get your workers to finish within a timely manner. This is where you have to take the assertiveness to give a hand and help your workers when they get backed up.

Those who are good managers are always being assertive and they are able to handle and take control of the situation. You need to make sure that you show your employees a firm voice and ethical role model. You need to be assertive and tell the employees what you expect from them and you'll find that you'll get what you want from your employees if you do everything with high ethics and respect.

If you are trying to be assertive, no matter what type of job that you have, you need to make sure that you always keep your ethics morally right and that you always show your employees respect. If you want your employees to work for you, you have to work with them. You want to make sure that you show your assertiveness to your employees and to your higher bosses. The minute you start showing some assertiveness you are going to get the employees to work with you and that higher-ranking co-workers recognize your hard work. Your assertiveness just might be the reason why you own the company someday. It is certainly going to be the reason why you get noticed at work.

Chapter 9- Assertiveness For Getting An Interview

It's hard when it comes to getting a new job, but it's mostly hard to face companies that won't even give you the interview. When it comes to the interview it is your chance to sell yourself. You don't want to miss the opportunity of showing the new possible employer that you are exactly what they are looking for.

The first thing that you will want to do when making the phone call is be pleasant, but firm. Do not use words like umm or like. You have to be direct in the reason why you are calling the business. You can start off promoting yourself, but most of the time you will only get the secretary who is going to pencil you in. This is why you need to give your name, the reason why you are going, and then ask them a question or two about the job. This way they already know that you are seriously interested in the job and that you are an assertive person who is going to get things done. Sometimes you are unable to call, but they would like to have you send a resume.

When you are sending a resume it can be anywhere between two to five pages long or however long it has to be to show them that you are fully qualified. You need to send a cover letter, even when it is not asked of you. Remember, the assertiveness will get you the interview. You will also want to sum important points up by using bold or italics. You don't want to rumble on about yourself, but you want to make it seem like you have something to offer to the company. They usually will browse through the resume; however, they will usually read the first and the last paragraph of the cover. This is because they want to know your name and what you can do for them. Don't use cheesy phrases for them to come to you for an interview, you will want to make sure that you get the interview by simply giving them an idea of what you are capable and what you plan to bring to the table.

It takes take much to get an interview, but it takes a lot to get a second interview. If you really want this job or just another job, you'll want to take the first interview to impress. You will want to boast all of your accomplishments to the interview and you'll also want to make sure that you start all of things that you have done that could benefit the company. You will want to leave the first interview by stating exactly what you can do for the company. You don't want to leave without putting your mark on the interview. The once the interview is over you will want to ask when call backs will happen, this will show some of your assertiveness to the interviewer, and then you will want to do a follow up call. Rather you get hired or called back for the second interview, you should at least ask for the address on where you can send the thank you card. By doing the follow up with a thank you card, the company will be more likely to call you when things fall through.

When it comes to being assertive in an interview, you don't want it to come off cocky. You can be assertive without being disrespectful. You will want to keep the conversation going and you want to be conversation about the things that you say or do, including your fashion statements.

CHAPTER 10- ASSERTIVENESS AND SAVING MONEY – MOTIVATION TIPS

When it comes to saving money you are going to have to learn how to be assertive and how to save and spent the money wisely. You will want to make sure that you always have enough money for the bills, a little bit for your savings, and a little bit for your splurging. You don't want to hold yourself back from spending a little bit of money here and there, but you have to be assertive and keep your control of the money's coming and going. You may first want to take the opportunity to consult a specialist. That means you have to go to a financial planner. You can meet a financial plan through the yellow pages or even through some websites. When you find a person who may be able to help you, you will want to gather up some of your bills and notices of your debts, as well as, your pay stubs. You will want to make sure that you get the right amount of debt compared to your actual pay checks.

When you go to meet the financial planner you will find that they will give you a list of suggestions. These suggestions will ask you if you are able to give some of your comforts up and trade some other comforts in for generic. If you start to take control of what you spend on common things like groceries, you'll be able to save a lot of money by only getting what you need and a few splurges.

To also save your money, the financial planner will tell you exactly what you need to put away money and they will also give you a small amount of money for your own disposal. Also, you may want to be assertive when it comes to saving money for your retirement. Those who are young have to learn how to save money for the long run and your financial planner will help you with your future.

If you feel like hiring a professional is too much, you can also use your own assertiveness and do all of the budgeting yourself. If you are going to be that assertive about your financials then you will want to take a lot of things in consideration. First, you need to think about the bills. What do you need to take home to keep the bill collectors at bay? Then think about what you would like to invest in. Maybe you need to save some money for an item, but you may just want to save some money for your future. You can make a lot of money by saving a little bit at a time. You would also like to look into things like saving for others. You may just find that your kids will be in college sooner than you'd like and you don't have much money saved for them. Expensive things may also come very sudden. There are a million other things that you could possibly need to pay for.

When it comes to finding reason as to why should become more assertive, you may just want to think about your future. Many people will save out of fear. There is a certain security when it comes to having a large savings. You don't ever have to worry about losing your house or other valuables. You also don't have to worry about the times when the unexpected happens. You are fully prepared for the future and you'll never have to worry about anything. Saving is very important and you may want to start saving soon so that you don't have to worry about the unexpected costs.

Chapter 11- Assertiveness And Relationships, Learning To Speak Your Mind

To speak your own mind you have to learn how to be assertive with your relationships. You can't just let the one person lead the relationship and you can't always be the person in charge of a relationship. You have to also realize that a relationship is a give and take. You will also want to find the assertiveness to speak your mind so that you can be open with your partner and the relationship can bloom even further.

You will also want to speak your own mind to your partner so that you can be happy with the relationship. When you hold things backs you will have things that will build up, but if you take the assertiveness to talk things out then you'll never have to worry about having repressed feelings. You'll never feel the need to have a sudden burst of anger for practically no reason. You have to speak your mind so that you two can have an honest relationship.

Some people who are in a relationship feel that they would rather have their feelings suppressed because of the fear of upsetting the other person, however, if you do not suppress your feelings but share them, you'll never have to worry about holding back again. You will enjoy being able to share your feelings and thoughts with someone who you have some to love. You will find a lot of comfort in the relationship because you can be totally honest and comfort with the person. When you take the assertiveness to speak your mind you'll be able to be yourself with the person. You won't have to worry about how they feel about you, because you'll know how they feel.

You will also want to learn how to speak your mind with the person who you want to spend the rest of your life with so that you two can have a relationship that works and will with stand the test of time. If you are willing to put the time and effort into the relationship, then it should be worth talking about. You will want to learn how you can speak your mind so that you can keep the communication flowing in the relationship. When the communication is flowing then you'll be able to understand each other, and you will notice that you'll fight less and less. For those who have a solid relationship, they will notice that it's only because you are able to keep the relationship in check.

You will find that the assertiveness for you to speak your mind in the relationship may just come to you or you may have to work on becoming assertive. You may just want to start yourself off by stating meaningless notations, but then you can work your way up to talking about your true feelings and how you would like to approach the future of the relationship. If you ever plan on having the relationship in the future you are going to have to learn how to become assertive and speak your mind about the relationship and how you feel.

You will want to take your time when it comes to expressing yourself and you'll also want to learn how to think before you speak. Those who choose their words wisely will be able to find the assertiveness to speak their own mind. It is important for your happiness for you to be able to get over your fears and open the paths of communication before you and your mate.

CHAPTER 12- ASSERTIVENESS AND BUSINESS, HOW TO STAY IN CONTROL

For those who are into business you have to learn how you can stay in control, even though it may be an extremely difficult task. You will find that sometimes you may not be able to keep your mouth closed when it is necessary. You need to find it in you to stay under control so you will suffer the consequences of your actions and words. You will find that you may even lose your job because you are not able to stay in control. It can be very difficult for you to work one day without blowing your stack. You need to keep your cool or you may end up losing a lot of respect and money. You may end up losing everything because you are unable to control yourself.

You need to go out of your way to control yourself because you need to make sure that you don't hinder your chances of making something of yourself in the business world. No one wants to deal with someone who can't stay cool when the heat is turned up. No one wants to be the partner of someone who flips out on a pin drop. No one wants to even be around someone who is unable to control themselves. This is the motivation that you should use to help yourself say in control. Even when it seems like everything is falling apart, you'll gain more respect by controlling yourself then you would if you fought the odds.

Once of the major reasons why you need to be assertive in staying control in business is respect. If you don't have respect in the business world you will never be able to make something of yourself or the company you represent. If you play by the rules and you take ethics and morals in every decision that you make, you'll be able to gain the respect of all of the others that you may have even doubted you. You'll never want to lose the control of one's self in the business room because it will damage not only the relationships that you have with your current coworkers, but future coworkers as well. You don't want to burn bridges too early. You should never lose the respect of others or you will end up in a very difficult position that you will wish that you never were in.

For the sake of making something out of yourself in the business world you will want to learn how to control the things that you say and do. This is because you are going to meet hundreds of people or company representatives that you may need to help you in the future. If you can learn to control yourself you'll be able to make a lot of valuable friends. The new friends will help you make it even further up the corporate ladder.

The only thing when it comes to trying to control yourself you may become even more frustrated. You may become disappointed with whom you become and often people associate this type of change with depression or the lack of care. The thing is that you can allow yourself to show your passion for something, but you also have to allow yourself to control the rage or fears that you may have. This is the difference between losing interest and helping yourself by controlling your actions and thoughts. You may also want to talk to others about your previous behavior and how you would like to change so that they don't make a big thing about the change; the way your co-workers react to you will help you to become a better person.

CHAPTER 13- ASSERTIVENESS TRAINING AND BUILDING CONFIDENCE

Being assertive does not mean that you have to be aggressive. It is going to mean that you live your life based on the belief that you have the right to be the way that you are. You have the right to your views and to express the way that you feel about things, needs, preferences or opinions. It is not going to mean that you are expecting to always get your own way and it is not something that gives you the right to be selfish.

Being assertive and getting the right training will give you confidence in who you are and the things that you do. You will have a better feeling about going out and talking in public and doing just about anything. We will not think anymore that we are less than someone else. We will know have the confidence to believe that we are just as good and that we have the right to express the way that we think and feel.

There are many people out there that have been subject to bad things in their life. They may have been abused, been depressed or just not very confident in themselves. This is something very serious and should be looked into. These people may just need a little bit of help with their assertiveness. Getting some assertiveness training is a good start to help fix the problem that is becoming hard to deal with in their life.

After you see how you can feel good about whom you are you will then realize that you are important and that you have a voice. Being heard is the most important thing because this will show that you have respect from others and that the way that you are feeling is important for others to hear about. You will not have to worry about being put down or feeling like you are not good enough anymore when you are in a crowd of people or even by yourself. The assertiveness training is going to give you the support and guidance that you are looking for to make you a strong and well-balanced person.

When you are not sure how to get the assertiveness training that you need, you can turn to a few different places. You can look online for some help in the subject. You will be able to get some tips and advice from the different sites that are dedicated to helping people become more assertive and get the things that are so important to them in life. With this great help, you will be able to work on your assertiveness as time goes on.

There are also great assertiveness training classes that you can take part in your area. These classes are for anyone that is looking to build their confidence levels and feel as if they are someone special. In fact when these people take the assertiveness training that is offered out there, they will see that they can be confident in whom they are and get some self-esteem that they were once lacking.

Having confidence in which you are will make it easier for people to go out and try new things. They will have the feeling that they can do anything and even if they fail, they will still know that they tried. Sometimes having the right assertiveness training for building confidence can totally reform a person into a more exciting and better citizen. Taking the assertiveness training classes is a good start for anyone to change their life for the better.

CHAPTER 14- ASSERTIVENESS TRAINING AND BUILDING YOUR SKILLS

Building up your assertiveness is something that you can do in many different ways. You can take on the challenge of making yourself feel better and have more respect for who you are. Getting to be more assertive will not make you a mean person. In fact, these training skills will make you a better person and one that is taken more seriously in life and it will give you a chance to build self-confidence and respect for whom you are.

Assertiveness training and building your skills is something that you can do for yourself. If you are looking to become good at something in life, you should think about what you can do to make this goal happen. You can do well for your life and make changes that you never thought were possible before. There is nothing wrong with wanting to be more exciting and have more skills to do the things in life that you have always wanted. With the right assertiveness training, you can now do this and so much more.

There are many things in life that depend on the way that we feel about who we are. If we are not sure what is holding us back, we may need to think about this question for a bit. For some, it may be the fact that they are not assertive enough. This may mean that they are not taking control of which they are and the things in life that mean so much to them. Having more assertiveness training may help a person take charge of their life and move on to the things that mean so much to then.

Being more assertive will also allow someone to feel important. This will give them the strength to move on and do the things that they want to in life. When a person is not sure of what their full potential is in life, getting some assertive training to help them recognize their skill may be the effort that they are looking for.

Do not sit back and let things pass you by because you feel you are not strong enough to do them. Life is short and you need to take charge now and maximize all of your full potentials. You are someone that can make things happen and with the right training; you can do just about anything that you want. It is ok to fail because you know that you have tried your best and put all of your efforts into it. This is all that you can ask for and in the end no matter if you are right or wrong, win or lose; you will feel good that you at least tried.

No matter who you are or what you are doing in life, you need to use your assertiveness skills. Being assertive is something that will help you stand up for who you are and all that you want to be in life. You may not feel like you have the confidence to do certain skills and things in life. If you are having these feelings, getting help from an assertiveness training course will help you get to where you need to be. You will start feeling great about yourself and you will want to get out there and try more things!

Building up your skills with your assertiveness training is one way to move up in life. You will have the strength to try your luck at new things and there is nothing that can hold you back in life. Being assertive is one of the best traits that you can have when you want to better yourself and the things that you do in life.

CHAPTER 15- ASSERTIVENESS TRAINING AND MANAGERS

If you are a manager you have to think if you are assertive enough in your communication skills to succeed in the things that you want to do. If you are struggling with your people skills or leadership's skills, you may want to have assertive training to help you along. Managers and supervisors must have the work skills and people skills that are necessary.

Your success is going to depend on their abilities to be assertive and use their communication skills as needed. Being in this position will require you to be ready for anything. You have to deal with certain types of people and take on certain situations that are not always easy. You have to know what you can do to be assertive and get through the ordeal out on top.

There are many great assertive training seminars that you can attend to help you along with these types of skills. You can get the help that you have been looking for to be more successful and get the respect that you are in need of from your co-workers and the people that you manage. You will also see a level or more respect and courteous from the people that are in charge of you as well. This is something that you should look forward to when you are thinking about taking a good course to improve your assertiveness.

You will learn how to do the following things from a good assertiveness training course.

You will be able to ask for and get the things that you need from your team. You will be able to get it done with the quality that is needed.

You will be able to deal with conflicts concerning employees, peers, and customers or bosses as well in a good and reasonable manner.

You can say no in a positive way and get your point across.

Build a good reputation that is going to make you well known for your good communication skills and saying the right thing in the right moment.

Getting the best out of difficult people - You will be able to show them that you are boss and that you are the lead.

All managers and supervisors will have strong communication and skills that will build a strong and important team. They will be able to learn how to be assertive and not be aggressive or passive at all. The course that teaches assertiveness training will help managers and supervisors with their customers and their employees. It will help them explore all sorts of issues and get them the help that they are in need of to be the best that they can.

Managers can also learn how to be assertive in the way that they can maximize their employees' potential and help them succeed as well. They can get them motivated and excited about learning things and doing what they are supposed to. There are so many great possibilities that you can do with your assertiveness training courses. You will be glad that you made the decision to get on board with a good assertiveness training course. Getting to take part in a good learning experience like this is going to maximize your earning potential and get you the leadership skills that you are looking for the most.

Your employees will also respect you more and give you the help that you are looking for in the business. You will be able to make your business succeed and grow more than you ever thought was possible. You will benefit from all the great learning powers you receive from the assertiveness training courses that you take.

ABOUT THE AUTHOR

I used to be a bit on the timid side which means I didn't say how I really felt about things; even if they were very important to me. I just wouldn't speak up. Looking back in retrospect, I had so many opportunities to say how I felt and would just keep my mouth shut. Well, that's changed.

I don't know if I got fed up enough or I just didn't want to be that way anymore (or a combination of both). After getting myself more focused mentally and really believing that the things I want to say is just as important as what someone else wants to say, things started to turn around for me in different relationships and work-related situations.

Now I feel that I can write about it and help others who are now the way I used to be. You too can break through just as I did. You'll start to feel so much better about yourself and wonder what took you so long to do something about it.

www.ingramcontent.com/pod-product-compliance
Lightning Source LLC
Chambersburg PA
CBHW071242240726
48654CB00009B/1167